What They Always Were

POEMS
Norita Dittberner-Jax

Minnesota Voices Project Number 68

New Rivers Press 1995

New Rivers Press is a non-profit literary press dedicated to publishing the very best emerging writers in our region, nation, and world.

The publication of *What They Always Were* has been made possible by generous grants from the Dayton Hudson Foundation on behalf of Dayton's and Target Stores, the Jerome Foundation, the Metropolitan Regional Arts Council (from an appropriation by the Minnesota Legislature), the North Dakota Council on the Arts, the South Dakota Arts Council, and the James R. Thorpe Foundation.

Additional support has been provided by the Bush Foundation, the General Mills Foundation, Liberty State Bank, the McKnight Foundation, the Minnesota State Arts Board (through an appropriation by the Minnesota Legislature), the Star Tribune/Cowles Media Company, the Tennant Company Foundation, and the contributing members of New Rivers Press. New Rivers Press is a member agency of United Arts.

New Rivers Press books are distributed by The Talman Company, 131 Spring Street, Suite 201 E-N, New York, NY 10012 (1-800-537-8894).

What They Always Were has been manufactured in the United States of America for New Rivers Press, 420 N. 5th Street/Suite 910, Minneapolis, MN 55401. First Edition.

For my people
the living and the dead

ACKNOWLEDGMENTS

What They Always Were took shape over an extended period of time and many people have helped along the way. Among them, I wish to thank poet and publisher C. W. Truesdale for his interest in my work; Monica Ochtrup, poet and editor, for the sustaining and crucial role she played in its final shape; Sharon Chmielarz, Barbara Sperber, Pat Barone, Mary Kay Rummel, and Carol Masters from Onionskin; poets and teachers Deborah Keenan, Alvaro Cardona-Hine, and Jim White. An Artist Fellowship from the Minnesota State Arts Board allowed me time away from teaching to develop some of the poems. Laura Beaudoin did the final editing.

Grateful acknowledgments to the editors of the following magazines and journals in which some of these poems first appeared, sometimes in earlier versions: *Commonweal, Frontiers: A Journal of Women's Studies, Hurricane Alice, Lake Street Review, Northern Lit Quarterly, Sidewalks, Sing, Heavenly Muse!,* and *Verve.*

"Crossing the River" will appear in *At Day's End* (National Library of Poetry Anthology, 1994); "Alone" (published as "A Single Space") appeared in *Looking For Home* (Milkweed Editions, 1990); and six of these poems appeared in *Border Crossings* (New Rivers Press, 1984).

CONTENTS

There is a moment in childbirth
when no amount of breathing helps,
when you finally understand
that you are the subject
of your own life,
and your situation is serious.

It happens again
over the years,
a hesitation before entering a room,
a failure of will,
the heart's temptation
to leave one chamber empty.

1. Leaving Home

IT WAS LIKE THIS

As a young girl it was like this—
slipping out of the cabin
in early morning
down to the dock, easing
the rowboat out
onto the Apple River,
rowing, the perfect intersection
of paddle and water,
muscles pulling in waves
not waking anything, not the fish
my father would catch,
not the life in the cabin (my mother
starting the oatmeal now)
not even wanting to waken myself
from this dream of water.

THE CHILD AT FOUR

Behind the colonnades, the only
architecture of the room, she sits
staring at the books
like pieces of sculpture.
She takes one out, feels the leather
the embossed gold,
as if it were braille and she
the diviner.

She knows the letters but not
the sounds. It is
impossible. She wants
to read the way her father does
crushing the newspaper in his lap
as he hollers out
to her mother the wonderful
terrible doings in the world.

Next year
when the leaves fall again and bedtime
comes early with the ceremony
of her mother reading
in the rocker,
after the summer games of blind-man's bluff

in that time

she will walk to school
in a new dress (the sashes
of the old ones will be mended).
When her mother presents her, no one
will know how serious this love is.
She will hide it,
her one gold coin
among so many coppers.

FAMILY REUNION, 1950

When you whisper
they don't stoop
down.

Uncles are more like trees.
You cross the grass,
climb up.

ST. VINCENT'S

Over the portal a merciful Jesus
and the words, "Suffer
the little children to come
unto Me."
We came, tripping over our names
like untied laces,
Arlene Pulowski
Frank Hovda
Norita Dittberner

The school itself was perfectly symmetrical,
the rooms a series
of quiet assurances.
We were told that you could walk into
a Catholic church anywhere
in the world and the mass
would be the same
so we never dreamed
of the Cathedral at Chartres,
never dreamed anything
that couldn't be ordered
from Montgomery Wards.

It might have ended that way
except for the principal
Sister Frances Carmel
who lodged like a sliver in the skin
stopping us in choir
until she drew from our voices
a perfect *kyrie*,
whose hands moved in arcs of music
large enough
to encompass us.

She was the irritation,
she knew how long it takes
to make a pearl.
At dismissal she'd stand like a duchess
at the portal
and let the lines of children pass through her
like acres and acres
of shimmering wheat.

WHAT GROWS WILD

Here, among the sweet-faced daffodils
stands the rhubarb,
spreading its rumors of flesh,
stalks whistling songs you never learned
in school,
making you remember a time
long ago or last week
when you held the core of night
in your hands.

It was July all summer,
nights of heat pressing the walls
of my parents' house,
you agreeing with everything
my father said,
about the freedom riders
about the war
about fishing.
We watched him doze,
the newsflash said, "Man sleeps
during ten o'clock news, can't last
much longer."
When the house was quiet with breathing
we left it for the tall grass
behind the clothesline
where our bodies opened
and sang with longing.

Chop it, dice it,
sweeten it with sugar,
make bread, cakes, pies,
roll them and roll them
as fast as you can,
rhubarb will be back
uncurling like a fist
into blossom,
stubborn as the body
which will not forget
the wilderness it knows.

LEAVING HOME

As the youngest of the girls,
growing up was a trunkful of formals
my sisters wore,
high heels hard as bone.
There was a party I remember.
The mirror was polished till the peonies
could see themselves
gathered up like children.
I sat halfway up the stairs watching my sisters,
Mary Lou at the piano
pounding out Gilbert and Sullivan,
Dorothy and Janet, full-skirted, laughing.

The sisters married, each in turn,
the house emptied of them.
Abandoned as a one-eyed cat,
I slept alone above the dining room
where my mother worked her crossword puzzles
and my father tallied his books.
They must have heard
how quickly I dressed, must have
seen me turn
to the stranger at the door
who smelled unmistakably
of blossom.

On the morning of my wedding,
I knelt by the buffet.
My mother held the prayerbook
with its cover of beaten wood
and together they blessed me in German.
I understood their hands on my head,
understood that I was leaving
one shore for another,
that the waters between would pass through
my own body.

REMEMBER THIS

I had forgotten
how it was to be awkward and full
the difficulty of turning
or rising from bed,
forgotten my own migration,
toward the end always listening
for the first sharp pain.

My mother told me a story.
When the pains came hard
she looked in the mirror
and seeing a woman
who would surely give birth
told her, "Today
you   will do   great things."

Toward the end I let
the body take over, one long
spasm, a tunneling
toward light.

TUESDAY

I am peeling potatoes
when you come home, stepping over
the shoes, coats,
the children's schoolbooks forgotten
in their hunger.

After supper
we talk about the foods our mothers cooked.
I didn't know
we had potatoes in common,
boiled and flaking
in a bowl of cracked china.

Outside, the wind crosses the yard
and shakes the back of the house.
You undress
and looking at your nude body
I say, "We look funny without fur."
"Yes," you answer,
"kind of plain."

Most nights we don't leap into bed
but come to it grateful
for a body that keeps on warming,
for the imprint of flesh
real as potatoes.

IN THE BEGINNING

Child, your head in my lap
is weighty with prospect—
what fire do you tend
that gives off such heat?

What day were you born?
the sixth day,
wasn't it?
What do you know?
day
night
fish
tree
each one a hand
parting the chaos.

Where are you going?
What sound makes you turn
toward the door
so I see your magnificent head
in profile
and the neck, backbone
holding it up
like a torch?

SEPTEMBER

At dusk
a rose-hipped sky
then darkness like a mother
pulling the shades.

The children bathed
new as the crayons, the notebooks
with their blue lines running
like dreams.

For the first time
in months
mothers, fathers
watch the news
but only half-listen.

They hear the child in sleep
stirring up
the old questions—
what if
I don't know the answer?
What if I get lost?

Tonight, mothers
fathers do not fight
or make love—
they are busy.
Even in their dreams
they prepare their offering.

ACROSS THE DRIVEWAY

for Helen Stokes

For weeks you don't see her
then one night
on the way to empty the garbage
you tell her everything.

She sends over the clothes
her children outgrow,
never entertains the same night you do
knowing you both
will need the ice bucket,
knows the state of your closets,
but won't tell.

When the trouble at her house
stops at the windowsill,
when some private grief overturns
the lawnchairs
you can wait.

Rituals of necessity connect you—
sooner or later
one of you will need eggs.

LEAVING EARLY

Why is the earth so indifferent?
A man dies early by thirty years
and the sky is placid as Buddha.
The streets don't buckle
in grief, water runs downhill
as always.

It only matters to humans
with the gift of memory.

There is no help for this.

HALLOWEEN

"The best ones are gone,"
the child says to her mother
at Knowlan's,
but they find one
with no soft spots
and an ample chamber for holding light.

The child carries in the pumpkin
which, like their Christmas trees,
has one bad side
flat, dirty from the ground.
"Never mind," says the mother
"Don't we all."

The child draws the face,
the mother carves the teeth
where the knife could so easily slip.
The sun stops playing in their yard.
"Light the candle,"
the child says.

The pumpkin leers—the knife
slipped.
The mother remembers her dead,
sees them walk crookedly
through the leaves.
Let them, she says to the child
with her eyes.
Let them.

AFTER DARK

Waiting for you to come home,
the street lights burning like votives,
and me, empty as a farmhouse,
its door flapping in the wind.

The weatherman says there'll be snow.
The sky is a warning of snow
held up, no one knows why.

WINTER

Why is it
that on Saturday night
the eye travels to apartment windows
and, seeing nothing,
imagines a life lived differently,
a room softly lit
appointments of brass
an alabaster cat whose jeweled eyes
must shine
clear through the night.

We have no room for imaginary cats.
You're out of work,
all your phone calls unreturned.
We make soup, clip coupons
living by the glare of too much light
our gaze focused always
on the prospect of surviving.

When it gets too bad
we leave the house and walk,
as we do now
with the cold coming down
like a malevolent god.

What we ask for is simpler than
money, a pocket of darkness
where a dream could grow
unwatched.

CONVERSATIONS AT THE END OF MARCH

On the boulevard
a patch of snow pulls away from the curb
drawing
to a final density

By late April
you won't notice what's left
a black tooth
rudimentary
and useless

Cranberries have the same habit
they dangle from their stems far into December
empty
except for their color
against the snow

Between seasons we remember
the remnants left
in the drawer
photographs
bookmarks
all smelling of absence and leather

Yesterday
when you opened it
each artifact testified
you listened
as if swimming in your first waters
you discovered gills
and almost turned back

BENDING TOWARD THE LIGHT

At baptisms, funerals
the mothers of my friends stand
like hot-house flowers
in their pews
hands palpable
as rain.

Husband,
when I get old, I will have my hair curled
for big occasions.

Imagine hair
the color of the Atlantic
blue in sunlight.

You with a cane
the carved head of a falcon
in your hand.

Imagine an age with nothing left
to deny.

Imagine
that we get old together.

AWAITING THE GIFT OF TONGUES

Mother,
seven years into your stroke,
I cross your silence the way I enter Monday morning
not seeing
until the picture of an African woman
in Sunday's paper
stops me.

Her face almost
breaks. She is caught in the moment
when birds suck in breath,
the lines of her mouth strained
from not singing.

How many times
have I seen the floodwaters rising in you
pressing for shape at your lips
words that never arrive
that dart in your hands
like lost fish?

ANNIE FISCHER

O Annie, where is your wig?
your glasses, your hearing aid?
the striped dress,
your pale sweater, Annie?
Where are you?

Do you remember your birthday?
the wine, the torte,
flowers bunched in your hand?

You don't remember do you?
not even who I am.
Your mind has closed, your body
seeks its own slow end,
the comfort of blankets
around your limbs.

O Annie of the good days,
my mother's sister,
last of those Fischers
who used to be called the best
dancers in Brown County,
is it like a poem?
Do you waken from your half-sleep
not knowing where you're going,
but hearing again the rumble
of wagon wheels on a dirt road
and the timothy grass swaying
like singers in the soft, soft wind?

A DEATH, ON YOUR MOTHER'S SIDE

We head West in the pick-up, leave behind
our children.
The box between us holds our good clothes,
newspapers,
a map marked in red.

Into South Dakota on a wide curve
you remember your mother,
how she drove into pheasants,
the blood-splattered feathers on the windshield,
Frances of the dark eyes,
of weekend trips back home,
your uncle's saloon, the revel
on Sundays while the roast beef burned
and you played blackjack
in the corner.

We enter the town like the ghost
of a parade. Ahead of us the wind uproots
a sagebrush and drives it down
a row of shops flat-faced
against the curb. There is no one
to ask directions.

We find your uncle in an unmarked house
on Main Street, a room of empty
folding chairs. He is small
in his coffin, he looks bad, you tell me,
as if something were still in the balance.

The family is gathered in a pocket
at the edge of town.
We sit in the yoke of the ceiling light,
caught in a day falling inward,
so much death, even the house is for sale.

I ask you with my eyes
why
we came.

Then familiar hands touch us.
In the kitchen, the counters are lined
with fluted cakes, sausages and ham.
Your cousin offers us whiskey.
Oh the stories we tell.

REQUIEM

It was the morning of my father's funeral.
I was standing behind you
in the bathroom,
you were parting your hair when I noticed
the small of your back,
vulnerable, cradled
between muscle and disc.

I wanted to rest there
or ask you, "Why don't we drive
to Red Wing today,
follow the Mississippi,
take our time, the two of us?"

Instead
I watched you teach our son
the intricacies of the Windsor knot,
turned to straighten
a daughter's collar and told the youngest
she did have to brush her teeth
for her grandfather's funeral.

Instead I put my head
into the wide mouth of sorrow.

I have never understood how
one moment, unable
to be contained, spills over
turning the whitest cloth
a deep indigo

and this moment is followed
by another so ordinary
commonplace as pennies.

How to honor both.
Let the ecstasy of the one
fire the eye
so we tell the truth
with our bodies

and how to let the common be—
helpful, functional,
moving time along,
a string of boxcars
full of grain.

2. Crossing the Time Zone

ALONE

The first nights after my husband moved out and the kids took
their turn at his house, I was alone for the first time in
my life. I stayed in our house, an old Victorian three-story,
not a house to wrap around you, but a procession of dignified
rooms strung out like time, a family house, but the family
had fled, and time cracked open.

I thought of myself as a statue, solitary and impassive.
I saw myself as the figurehead of a ship, the kind my husband
and I had seen years earlier in Boston harbor. During the
day, as I went about the frantic task of reorganizing everything
from my soul to my closet, the image of the woman, braced
against wind came to me often.

Nights were worse. I bought an old bookcase headboard and
mattress from a neighbor for $25. I lined up the books that
I loved above my head. These seemed a kind of lifejacket
I put on before I entered sleep.

Turning out the light, I curled up in the corner, the way
an infant finds a place to curl in a crib. I seemed to split
in two then, one part of me heavy, exhausted, welcoming the
oblivion of sleep; the other, the figurehead, rising above
the bed, the roof of the house, the city, the country, to
consider my position in the world. What spatial claim was
mine, now that I was just one person occupying a single space
in a double bed? Was I held in God's eye or no eye at all?

I was so close to the child of seven, writing on paper in
large block letters, 296 Thomas Avenue, St. Paul, Minnesota,
U.S. of A., Western Hemisphere, Earth, the Universe.

UPON HEARING OF THE DEATH OF AUNT RUTH

Memories of her swoop down overwhelming me. The longing I
have to be the young mother again with Aunt Ruth at my table
and three kids fighting to sit next to her takes possession.
One last meal: Let it be Thanksgiving.

Crank the meat grinder, pulverize oranges and cranberries.
Baste the turkey, where is the knife sharpener? Jessica,
wash your hands! The doorbell's ringing! Eric races Emily
to the door and opens it. Ruth and Keith come in, carrying
pumpkin pies and Jell-o, wrapped in immaculate white towels.
Potatoes boil on the stove giving off bursts of steam; Lee
carves the turkey, I unmold the Jell-o with fruit cocktail
which the children think is the fanciest of foods. Eric asks
Ruth where she's going to sit. Jessica says quickly, "I get
the other side." Emily sobs, having lost the race to the
door and sitting by Ruth. But Ruth whispers in her ear that,
really, the person who sits across from her has the best view,
so all through the meal, Emily sits on her chair, boosted
by the St. Paul and Minneapolis telephone books, beaming across
the turkey at Aunt Ruth.

The vision fades as quickly as it came. I am sitting at my
desk, forty-seven years old. The house is perfectly still.

LIFELINE

I sit at my desk as if it were the sickbed
of an old friend. I straighten and clean;
then I read what I wrote yesterday;

> There are no words
> willing to come out.

In the back drawer, I find a small stack of
index cards with odd snippets of poems.

> Am I Winter, that my children flee
> like geese? In a hundred ways they
> tell me of the end of their childhood.

Handwritten, my former words, small
indigenous poems cut close to the bone.

> I have been lucky this year.
> Birds nest in my house;
> none of my people have died.

This is how the poems began. In the middle
of living, words erupted like rock in our
Wisconsin soil.

> I have as much trouble as ever.
> Monday reeked of failure, but
> on Tuesday the tulips opened.

The woman who wrote those words knew
when to write and when to live. She did
not brood.

Tonight, a full moon rises
over supper dishes—chicken bones
blessed in new, blue light.

The woman who wrote those words knew
how to keep things small, knew that words
are not life, but the melody you hum while
you're living it, footstep, heartbeat,
your own slow breath.

MOVING

To be this clean
palms empty and open
the day sunny
flat as a movie set
my house uncluttered
ready for sale
the children taller than I
going, soon gone
all my rooms unpeopled
as if someone
had gone on ahead
cleared a path through
forever.

AWAY FROM HOME

You still don't understand, do you?
Wandering the streets of Casselton,
Browerville, (where am I?) though you're tired
and your hips ache, still you continue,
another errand, a quarter for the newspaper,
a spoonful of time drawn out like the last train.

    Not to be known, not touched,
    the air a wall around me,
    the tall windows of loneliness,
    the strange hairdos, the ties
    on men I do not know,
    how I would welcome the dog
    who sleeps on a pile of clothes
    at home.

    I know precisely how long
    I can stand my room.
    I have measured the hours
    against the white beast crouched
    in the corner.

Listen to me!
You, estranged from yourself,
short-sighted turtle looking for home,
be home to yourself.
Be balm to cells, blood,
your orphaned legs,
your lonesome sex.

Breath in.
Draw into yourself the world—
barn
cafe
stranger
Breath out.

Let your reserve fall away.
Stay with the beast hour after hour, then
don't come home all night
but for God's sake enter into
your life.

NEWS BRIEF

I read in yesterday's paper that
in the Sudan, the refugees are so weak
they can't fight off the hyenas
plucking at the bodies of their dead
relatives. I only wanted a quick
once-over to keep myself informed.
I have a bridal shower to give,
a hundred things to clean and hide.
Emergency food has been sent
to the region, but most of it is not
reaching the refugees because of
the political situation. Everyone
is coming, my sisters and cousins,
ten nieces, not counting the bride;
I've ordered the centerpiece,
tulips and hyenas. Neither officials
of the Sudan nor neighboring Ethiopia
could be reached for comment.
If the news account had been more abstract,
the shower would be perfect,
right down to the mints. As it is,
I'm planning a quieter celebration
because of the death in the family.

TULIPS

My son gives me tulips for my birthday.
I arrange them
in a clear glass vase,
their thick stems rushing toward morning,
toward blossom,
tulips at my elbow
on the table
in front of mirrors where they keep bursting
into yellow and red
into what they always were.

PORTRAIT: JESSIE AT SIXTEEN

She arrived in a squall
of hunger,
second child.
Took my breast
in hands pink, fierce
then let it fall away
just to laugh.

I see little
of myself in her
only the hips set wide
as sentries
to guide the generations
out safely.

Where did she come from
this one who threw
her head back
at the piano
to see if she could play
the minuet blind
and how fast?

In all that
Northern European blood
what was hidden from me
from her father
that she should shimmer
like a gypsy,
skirts falling in folds
of magenta, of gold,
dark eyes quickening
like castanets?

LOVE LETTERS

It is the quietest thing they've done
in years. Behind closed doors, on summer
afternoons, my daughters write letters
to young men. Paper disappears
from my desk; there is a run on stamps.
Fat letters to an airman apprentice
in Pensacola, pastel envelopes
to the drummer at music camp.

Slow summer afternoons of overcast skies
and deep humidity. My daughters in their
idleness watch soap operas and file
their nails while they wait for the mail,
the pattern of days so set, that when
my son hears from Rose in Honolulu,
after an absence of two years,
he asks for stamps.

Summer nights, my daughters fall asleep
to the strum of crickets and the whispers
of absent lovers. They waken, their faces
bright as peaches in the bowl of morning,
another day, another summer day, dozing
like cats in the sun, another promise,
write soon, write soon.

THE LILIES

Through difficult weeks
you bring me armsful of lilies
from the farm.
Their stamens stain my clothing
a scattering of lily dust
like your blessing on me.

So that what I remember afterward
between the white padded room
of withdrawal and the house deathly clean
are the lilies, and you across the table,
the bouquet between us.

There, where the lilies part and fall,
your face appears
bearded with lilies
as if they were holding you
in flaming hands.

PLAINSONG

For E.J.J.

I walk tonight
among the trees, damp
at the river's edge,
the road thin as the song
of a flute.

At the shoreline
a Hmong family fishes
for supper.

A dog barks—
the woman wraps her skirts
closer, huddles
with her children.

She is from the other side
of the world
where you are now
among the orphans.

The family gathers up
the fishing poles
passing through reeds
on quick feet.

If they had stayed
I wouldn't feel your absence
so.

In their wake
the sky, the only bridge
between us, shuts down
goes home.

CROSSING THE TIME ZONE

Today, I counted—
fifty-seven days until we marry.
Soon it will be thirty
then nine, too short
for arrangements, too long
for the heart.

Why must the days be so orderly?
Monday always followed by
Tuesday. What a string of acolytes
they are, formal and slow
the light held steady
in their hands. I bow
to them, make an affliction
of phone calls,
clean my closet. My clothes
are waiting
in a terminal fifty-seven days long.

But inside I have already scattered time,
scooped it up
flung it until it surrendered
like a flag at my beckoning.
In my mind we have already arrived
under an arch.
You are holding my hand as you do,
we are peaceful as rain
on a November morning.

THERESA'S BAR

Q: "What kind of farming
do you do?"
A: "I wouldn't be farming
at all except for my son.
He died."

Three years ago now
but for Russell
the news is fresh as spring dirt.
He so full of his son's death
the words spill over, leak out
and I can see by his eyes
that he has been summoned again
to the field where the tractor overturned
on the boy.

You return with our beer. We talk
the three of us
about the death. Russell's face reddens
as he speaks of leaving
the farm, the memory.
Your arm is braced against the wall.
I stand in that arc in the field
of your radiation
drawn to it out
of the cold.

All day I have moved between heat and cold.
This morning I inched my chair closer
to the fire as the day collapsed
into rain. Then when it cleared
I rode Bea through the woods,
braced my legs against her belly
and felt in her stride
the blaze of motion.

Now Russell asks me to dance.
We swing to the music of tuba
accordion. His arms lift
to the music, "I remember the night
and the Tennessee Waltz."
He tells me which halls
had the best dance floors before
they burned down.

When you and I dance, Russell disappears
toward the bar where Theresa
fills his glass and the crosses she wears
in her ears flash
by bar light.
We move, we don't talk.
It is a month to the eve
of our wedding. Move, love
don't talk.
We are the fire
around which terrible stories are told.

I've resumed
my old life
of balance,
walk the dog
down the parkway
of perfect
lawns, and feed
my stomach
the food it knows,
carrots, oatmeal.

Where are
the mountains
to draw the eye up,
the excavations
down
into other lives?

Here,
on the Great Plains
I live
on a band
of earth thin
as a child's
drawing,
one line
for the ground,
one house,
one tree.

How I miss you,
Mexico,
your thin
dogs,
your tilting
cathedrals.

3. To See the World

CATARACTS

A smudge on the lens, dirty fingerprints
on glass. I examine my eye for outward
signs, but nothing shows. The loss is silent
and insidious as fog: the finches on the fencepost,
berries on the mountain ash, every day the list
gets longer, as I lose the particulars
of the world.

Worst of all, I lose the articulation
of shadow and light. Darkness is a mute thing
that no longer speaks to me in tongues.
On summer nights, when shadows gather in the trees,
I don't see the braid they weave. What I see
is one vast absolute.

And entering some rooms, I startle
the way an infant does, unprepared
for the abundance of light pouring in
from the windows. I shield my eyes
the way the holy women do in pictures
of the Resurrection, and turn away,
as they do, from perfect, stunning light.

VISION

Where does this thirst come from, to see?
More than my eyesight, more than
curiosity, I take such pleasure
in the city's composition, cold metal
flush up against brick and leaf,
the endless detail, shabby, glorious.

An old woman from the high-rise shuffles
down the ramp, then eases into
a natural step. What does she see
this morning? Fear of falling?
Arthritis in her spine? Is the pattern
of architecture a mirror of her life?
Is the old World Theater the war
with a hundred recesses, and the darkened
stone the death of her husband?

I am looking at myself thirty years
from now and seeing all the places
where my life intersected with history,
the small life always hidden with the large.
The spire of the church is the death
of a beloved, and the new office tower
the thirst to live still more, and the trees,
the lovely city trees, where birds rest
between flights, these are my own death
unripened.

WEST SEVENTH STREET

This section of the city is dedicated to repairs
used appliances
rebuilt transmissions.
By-products of beer pour
from the smokestacks at the brewery.
At every corner its lineage is tacked:
Old Fort Road begat
West Seventh. The hooves of cattle beat
this ground. This street still
has the heart muscle
of an ox.

The busdriver knows it, see
how he turns the wheel with one finger?
This is his run more
than the skyways downtown unbuttressed
by dirt.

He learned the blunt edge of the knife here
the language of plumbers
who name their parts male and female
because one fits into
the other.

Today he watches for spring four times
twice uptown
twice downtown.
It squints off the bits of glass, rises
in a breeze off the river,

the river so close
he forgets
living here
that before the oxen
was the river,
flicking its tongue at the land.

EISENBERG'S FRUIT COMPANY

The cantaloupe are in, he says
drives a wedge into the crate,
the wood
gives.

In his hands
he holds the weight of melon,
wipes the knife
on his belly, the rind
splits.

He laughs.
The melon halves sway
easy as rowboats.

SAUERKRAUT SUPPER

For Maryann Turner

In honor of my birthday, you ask me
to the sauerkraut supper at St. Adalbert's
in Frogtown, my old neighborhood.

We meet in the church basement, line up
with the others, large men and women
who lack confusion about who
they are, who live by rules
of beer and coffee, who drinks it,
who pours it.

We are all happy to be here,
moving in line to the kitchen
where the cook raises the lid and steam
rises like a genie.

She ladles the sauerkraut into great bowls;
other women pass us carrying platters
of roast pork, bowls of potatoes and
applesauce, baskets of bread, apple pie,
a feast of pale foods.

There isn't a green for miles, no broccoli,
no zucchini, those foreigners in
the new land, nothing sharp, nothing to vex
our souls that have traveled so far
from our starched childhoods, as if

we had all pushed our chairs back
from the table and vanished, years ago,
leaving our ghostly mothers with the dishes.

LAKE COMO

Lake Como. In the northern hemisphere
of the world egg. I have come here
all my life. I walk around the lake
to see the concordance of ducks and
geese; the concerts in the pavilion
with Max Metzger directing the Sunday
afternoon orchestra; we took the children
to the zoo here when they were small,
and all three of them harassed the giant
turtle who dragged himself through
the lion house; before that I slipped
through the high school crowd at Como
dances just to put myself directly
in Dan Zechmeister's line of vision;
and even further back, in the baby book
my mother kept, this entry under
BABY'S FIRST OUTING, "When baby Norita
was two weeks old, Dad took her out
in the car to Como Park; they stayed
about an hour. She slept all the time."
He must have held me. Each scene, each
memory is perfect, as if Como Park and
St. Paul were inside an Easter egg ruffled
with frosting. I see inside that the sky
is the blue of the morning glories climbing
the back porch in Frogtown. The streets
are straight and no one suffers alone.

THE NUN'S HANDS

If I had taken the freeway to the doctor's office, I wouldn't
have seen all this, Frogtown in early spring, dirty and poor.
The seedy mortuary where I wanted to be buried from, the spire
of St. Vincent's, the school boarded up. I'm not surprised
that the neighborhood of my childhood is gone, but that even
the neighborhood of my parents' last years has disappeared
depresses me this morning.

I wait in the doctor's office for him to confirm my fears:
cataracts worsening, a loss of detail, every room I enter
smudged. Around me are the old people who share my disorder
and much worse: a daughter shepherding her blind father,
and two nuns, one in a wheelchair and the other her inevitable
companion.

The nun in the wheelchair lists sharply to the left, her body
juxtaposed to itself. She is dressed in pastels; her white
hair is short and covered by a small veil, the only remnant
of the old habit. Her eyes don't track, but there is a certain
cunning in them, a remnant of her mind. In the list and angles
of her body, she reminds me of my mother in her last years.

Her companion adjusts the wheelchair and then settles into
her seat. Immediately, she takes out of her bag a rectangular
piece of plastic grill. She threads a large needle with red
yarn and deftly weaves it up and down between the holes.
She is making a decoration, an ornament, perhaps for the
parish boutique. She does not glance at the sister in the
wheelchair or at me. She is lost in her project, quickly
finishing row after row.

Her useful hands move up and down, up and down. Her hands are rocking up and down. I watch her, mesmerized. She seems to say, "See child? Up and down, up and down; repetition is the key. Set yourself a rhythm, then stick to it. Up and down. What can you do about the world anyway? Up and down, up and down."

MAKING MYSELF SMALL

For the surgery,
I make myself
very small.

My breath
comes deep and slow.

I compose my body
into a landscape
out West
where the foothills
of the Rockies begin.

I fold my toes
and cup my hands
into each other.

My whole body,
a long afternoon
with only the slightest
of winds.

I am so quiet and small
I almost disappear

the only disturbance
the monitor bouncing
its inane ball
off my regions

from peak to peak,
the news, how I
go on.

THE FIRST DAY: WHAT SHE SAW

Bricks!
red tile roof
the intricate design of the wrought iron fence
pine needles
the trim on houses
labels
street names
speed limits
black print in books
ears
buds on trees
broken glass on the sidewalk
the exotic pattern of the coleus leaf
We the People on the Declaration of Independence
a wart
the minute hand on the clock
dresser pulls
the stars on the flag
Over 75 million served at McDonald's
the make-up of gravel
the white feather of the sparrow
the eagle on the mailbox
the dog's toenails
stars!

IN THE GARDEN

Stunned by the world so newly green,
the leaves layered in shadow and light,
I walk among the flowers beautiful
as bells and the willow's green rain.

Blossom after blossom breaks open,
their names a rush of sound
in my throat. Am I Adam
that I should want to name
each one so? Daffodil, lilac,
tulip, hyacinth, trillium,
columbine, bleeding heart,
bloodroot.

Underneath their beauty, thunder.

At night I dream a whale thrashes
inside me, something wild
let loose in the world.

CROSSING THE RIVER

We leave Sunday, drive 61 north,
follow the Mississippi River upstream
through Winona and Lake City, river towns,
and between, the rising of the bluffs.

We stop to see the Whistling Swan encamped
in the backwaters, everywhere white and alive
with disagreement. They have crossed the river
on their way to Chesapeake Bay.

We have crossed the river ourselves, left behind
your small mother ailing in the hospital.
I feel my own mother very near, her life
and death contained like a seed in me.

I keep my eye on the parting of water from land.
This is where God got the idea for river;
this original landscape is the valley of
myth and dream.

We thread our way home between river
and bluffs crouched like fierce buffalo.

LEVITATING TOWARD DULUTH

I watch for the first pine, a flag of the country ahead,
and listen for the knock of geography shifting gears,
land rising out of bedrock and farm field.

Everything around me appears ordinary,
but inside I am waiting to be conducted
through something grand.

We climb higher, a long string of cars
crossing the St. Louis River, cutting through
the last elevation, then on to the top.

Suddenly the lake, huge and primal,
hidden behind the hunched shoulders of the hills
and with it the ships, bridges, and railroads,

all the commerce of water and land.
For a split second, we shimmer like trout
in the great flow of it, each bay and pier,

then shoot downhill into the stone channels
of the freeway, all our climbing released,
and arrive on the other side

of the city and onto the North Shore,
quiet now, we are inside geography,
we hum along, a string of cars

whose passengers turn naturally
to the thin line between water and sky
where all our hopes gather.

ON THE PLANE

Suddenly a clearing of fierce blue,
clouds spin off like fine wool,
a great arm of beach and the sea
unbroken, wishing itself on the land.

Where are the grids, the roads,
the orderly segmentation of land
divided like apples in a math book?
Who said it took six days to make the world?

An act of passion made this fine stew
of sea, land, sky, one overflowing into
the other, a whirling of elements.

Big Bang or God, neither with a straight eye,
sent rivers weaving through land like drunks.
Straight lines are for accountants.
We live on one great exalted curve.

ON THE BUS TO MEXICO CITY

We weave from mountain
to mountain, your body leans
into mine and mine into yours;
in the front of us, in the back of us,
it is the same, this sweet
sashay, this rocking

at the top of the world, a samba
on the radio, the driver calm and heavy,
the babies asleep in their mamas' arms,
all of us close, folded into each other
like mountains.

THE SEA

I can't
get over the great
green weight of it,
the heft and feel
of the water, pitching
me forward, throwing
me back, wave after
rocking green wave,
salt in my mouth,
playing and rolling in
water, first water,
happiest of waters,
mother and father
of waters, pulling in,
flowing out, the tide,
the pull and roll
of the sea.

THE OLIVE TREES

When we drove into the Alentejos,
the flat dry land in the middle of Portugal,
the grass was bleached the color of straw
and everywhere I looked: olive trees
broad as peasants and flat on top
as if sun and sky weighed too heavily.

I remembered van Gogh's painting of olive trees
and was shocked at how exact his eye was.
I thought the waviness was all technique,
but his vision was *accurate*. Those trees
could hold no more.

CHAMBRE

We walk the town
before the shops close
for the long silence of Sunday,
but something is already lost
to us. A wind rises up from the
mountains and whirls us back
to the hotel.

A gray room, substantial
and plain, a bed dressed
in white, sheets and bedspread
white on white; a small sink
in the corner; a bidet curved
like a baby's bath or a violin;
a small desk under the window.

The window: Large, shuttered,
draped in dark brocade and
on the interior, layers
of delicate sheers.

You are sick, dizzy.
I pretend to write at the desk
thinking how to get you home
if the jig is up, Guarda
to Lisbon, Lisbon to London,
London to Minneapolis and home.

Under the white sheets we dream
and turn in sleep and dream
and turn in sleep and dream.

In the morning, you are better.
We uncover the windows, draw back
the curtains, and light pours in
turning the hollow where we slept
and even our bodies into bowls
of light.

When you die and I am alone,
at the end of my life, all the rooms
we slept in on the road will be
reduced to this one chamber.
Bed. Desk. Window. Light

POET'S CORNER, WESTMINSTER ABBEY

After the overstuffed chapels, the corridors
narrow with the tombs of forgotten lords,
an opening of white marble, a widening of air
that leaves enough room for thought:

> *The communication of the dead*
> *is tongued with fire beyond*
> *the language of the living.*
> (T. S. Eliot)

In the small library of epitaphs in stone
I read the legacy of words from which I trace
my origins, back to the overheated classrooms
in Frogtown where I first heard these voices:

> *The first condition of human goodness*
> *is something to love; the second,*
> *something to reverence.*
> (George Eliot/Mary Ann Evans)

These voices wash through me, a river
that runs underneath all the writing.
To fit the object perfectly with words,
to articulate the soul's lonely odyssey
in the world,

> *Time held me green and dying*
> *Though I sang in my chains like the sea.*
> (Dylan Thomas)

to break silence and go back to silence,
this is the work I want to do
day after day after day.

> *With courage to endure*
> (The Brontë Sisters)

FLYING HOME

Hour after hour, airplane windows
strung with garish beads of sunlight.
Layover in Boston, stand-by in Chicago.

Now, at last, night comes on in her mercy.
The steward dims the lights; we settle
into a low hum.

I am floating in a dark, watery world,
an aquarium, a womb; I am quiet as a fish,
passing through space.

I breathe in and out, my eyes large,
unblinking. I move and see.
The world.

I remembered you today, Ma
as I stood by my sink
examining the sky.

How patiently you always
explained how we'd know
if the picnic were on:

"If there's enough blue
to cut an apron out,
the day will clear up."

Looking up at the sky
I imagine an apron blue
as a whale,

sashes sailing on the wind
like kite tails.

How is it where you are?
You, folded so long
into your death—

there's been no word
for years. Here
water runs off plates,

the furnace kicks in
like a great heart.

ABOUT THE AUTHOR

Norita Dittberner-Jax, the sixth of seven children, was born and raised in the Frogtown neighborhood of Saint Paul, Minnesota. A graduate of the College of Saint Catherine's, Ms. Dittberner-Jax has long been active in the writing community—as a writer-in-the-schools for COMPAS, as a writing specialist and teacher for the St. Paul Public Schools, and as an active member of the Loft. She taught literary arts at the Minnesota Center for Arts Education. Ms. Dittberner-Jax has won a Loft Mentor Competition, a fellowship from the Minnesota State Arts Board, and a Travel and Study Grant from the Jerome Foundation. She has three children, is married, and lives in Saint Paul.

ABOUT THE COVER ARTIST

The painting on the front cover of *What They Always Were* is by Joyce Lyon, a visual artist living in Minneapolis, whose work often centers on the experience of place. Her artist's book, *Conversations with Rzeszow*, was published in 1993 with the assistance of a Jerome Book Arts Fellowship. Twice the recipient of a Minnesota State Arts Board Fellowship, Ms. Lyon has had solo exhibitions at Soho 20, Artemisia Gallery, and the Tweed Museum and in many regional galleries.